You've Got to be Kidding!

Cookie Leonardelli

authorHOUSE®

AuthorHouse™
1663 Liberty Drive
Bloomington, IN 47403
www.authorhouse.com
Phone: 1-800-839-8640

First published by AuthorHouse 9/13/2011

ISBN: 978-1-4567-9607-5 (sc)
ISBN: 978-1-4670-2690-1 (e)

Printed in the United States of America

*Any people depicted in stock imagery provided by Thinkstock are models,
and such images are being used for illustrative purposes only.
Certain stock imagery © Thinkstock.*

This book is printed on acid-free paper.

Introduction

Some people are born into this world with an emptiness that seems never to be filled. Their lives are a journey different from many others, yet in the telling of their stories, their tale rings true for many.

I'm one of those tale bearers and this is the story of part of my journey. In reflecting on many of my experiences, I can only call this compilation, "You've Got to be Kidding!"

My prayer for you, the reader, is that you'll find healing as you read, or if you are in the small population that hasn't had to seek healing, an understanding of those who do.

"It's like this: When I was a child, I spoke and thought and reasoned as a child does. But when I grew up, I put away childish things. Now we see things imperfectly as in a poor mirror, but then we will see everything with perfect clarity. All that I know now is partial and incomplete, but then I will know everything completely, just as God knows me now."

~ 1 Corinthians 13:11, 12 ~
NLT

I heard him before I saw him. "How're you doin there, George? What's goin on with that sheep of yours? You want me to come over, see what I can do?" The crowd seemed to thin out as he approached. Sort of like the manor in which we see the parting of the Red Sea. I'd estimate he was 6'10" with cowboy hat and boots and as he approached, my friend leaned toward me and said, "I want to introduce you to my Uncle Rufus (fictitious name)". I approached this meeting with a tiny bit of trepidation. This giant of a man in this farming town didn't seem like someone who'd embrace a woman in leadership in the church.

"Uncle Rufus, I'd like you to meet my pastor. This is Cookie and she pastors the church we belong to."

"You married?" Rufus inquired as he sized me up and down until I felt like a heifer at a county fair.

"Yes, sir, I am." I replied.

"What's wrong with your husband let you do a fool thing like take a man's job?"

"There's absolutely nothing wrong with my husband, he's in ministry with me and is the other half of our Sunday morning worship service. He leads worship, is an elder in our church and fully supports me in ministry." Why do I feel the need to defend the call God placed on my life? My voice is getting louder and I'll have to bring that back down to "meek", or he'll peg me as a bra burning liberal and discount anything of value I may have to say.

"Well, I don't believe in women pastors", Rufus announced. What a huge surprise this was to me as you can well imagine. Putting a (what I hoped looked like a sincere) church lady face on, I smiled warmly and replied,

2

"well thank goodness for my fellowship and for me ... God does!"

It wasn't a dream of mine to become a pastor. When I was small I wanted to be a bulldozer or an Indian chief. I probably picked a bulldozer because as the youngest of three children growing up in an abusive alcoholic home, I dreamed of power...power to make everything all right... power to plow all the fear, pain, and heartache under. The Indian Chief was because I thought their headdresses were really cool. A brother in my church recently told me that as far as he could see, I'd achieved both those dreams. As a bulldozer I push against demonic forces that would attempt to place themselves above God and as an Indian Chief in my position as Senior Pastor of Rio Rancho Foursquare Church. But no matter how you cut it, I never aspired to the ministry. Fifteen years ago I believed that only men should hold positions of authority in the church. It was the death of my nineteen year old daughter and the resigning of my then Pastor (as well as the prayers of some mighty men of God) that placed me in the position that I now hold. Since that time my views and my heart has changed dramatically. It's the circumstances of that change that I hope to place on paper here, to encourage some, to correct some, and to enfold some in the arms of a God who is far bigger than our petty differences and far holier than our meager attempts at spirituality.

It was summer camp at Lone Tree Bible Ranch and our youth group was sitting in the evening service. At the time I was the Youth Pastor and Assistant

Pastor of our church. I don't know if you've ever had the experience, but summer youth camp was, for the teens, one fun filled week of events that was supposed to put Jesus first in their lives. For myself and my youth staff...all volunteers, it was one sleep deprived week full of "why are you hiding in the bushes with her?" and "no you can't go take a nap in the cabin during service" kind of situations. It was the second or third night and the speaker looked around the partially darkened gym as though he was looking for an opportunity to share an earth shattering idea. [For those readers that believe in the gifts of the Spirit operating in these days, it was a word from our Lord. For those who don't, it was a really good idea that for some unknown reason planted itself in the speakers mind.] I was sitting in the back, leaning against the wall and trying not to fall asleep (remember, it was the teens opportunity to hear from God) because I am not the type of person that can go through many sleepless nights and still appear "spiritual". In my early years as a Christian I would force myself to appear engrossed in whatever was being shared when in reality, I was doing my grocery list in my head. As a side note, I think it's a shame that we worry so much about how we appear to others and not nearly enough about how we appear to God. But I digress, back to the story. I felt a stirring in my stomach; you know, the shaky "heads up" kind of feeling that tells you something big is about to happen?

"You, back there by the wall..."he said. I of course looked around at those sitting by me and tried to determine who exactly "you" was. When he didn't break eye contact I pointed to myself with the "you couldn't possibly mean me" gesture and he shook his head to show that yes in fact, he did mean me. Now most people would do a little jig inside at the sheer excitement of being singled out by God, but I was more concerned that for some unknown reason God was suddenly going to show this congregation of people who I really was. You see, I still hadn't let go of smoking...cigarettes, not weed...and I was terrified that my Christian façade would crumble and people would figure out that I wasn't perfect like everyone else. Never the less, the word for me began to tumble from him and everything inside of me got a big "heads up".

"You've been journaling for a long time now all of your thoughts and feelings and God wants you to use your journals to write a book that will bring healing to many." He stopped and let that start to sink in. "The Lord wants you to acknowledge this word He's given you." And he waited for a response from me.

You know how it is when someone makes an unpleasant sound and everyone turns to stare at the offender? Well that was how it was then. I sat there like a dummy that could not quite comprehend English. My sister in Christ, Sherry, turned to me with the "you are making a fool of yourself" look on her face and she jabbed me in the side once, hard...and then again. Being the spiritual giant that I am I responded to this new life direction from the creator of Heaven and Earth with a nod. A nod! Okay, so I'm not the giant I wanted to appear to be. And over the next ten years or so I continued to tell myself that I would get to that real soon. The problem was that other than the usual pain and heartache life throws at you, I didn't think that I had anything of value to share. Bottom line…if I wouldn't want to read this book, then why should anyone else want to? And then, true to the Almighty God that He is, my life took some very drastic turns that shook my faith to its absolute core.

"For I can do everything with the help of Christ who gives me the strength I need."

~ *Philippians 4:13* ~
NLT

When I was small, I had a best friend named Sally Mippy. She always did the right thing, or almost always, and everyone wanted to be around her. I considered myself most fortunate that she spent all her time with me. She had long, golden curls and crystal blue eyes and even as she grew older she remained very petite. Her dresses were perfectly starched with pinafores that never revealed even a hint of gravy that was once dribbled on the perfect white landscape. Pristine…Sally wore white lace tights and shiny black patent leather shoes on holidays like everyone else, but on regular play days as well. Her world was perfect. Sally's dad didn't try to kill her mom when he was drunk. Sally's dad didn't drink and he always smelled like English Leather cologne. Sally wasn't fat, lazy, stupid, ugly, or unplanned and unwanted. She mattered. This perfect child was born of my imagination and being everything that I would never be, she validated my very existence.

Since honesty is the best policy, I feel it's only appropriate to admit to the fact that Sally actually wasn't the one who ate all the freshly baked peanut butter cookies for the women's cookie exchange (although she was hiding under the bed with me as we consumed all four dozen delectable treats). To this day peanut butter cookies remain one of my absolute favorites. Sally wasn't the one that took my sister, Kathie's new dress and wore it for play when Kathie was at school. Sally didn't really wet the bed every night until she was eight…that was me. But it wasn't on purpose! I always dreamed that I had gotten up and gone into the bathroom. The problem was that each and every morning I awoke to the knowledge that I hadn't in fact gotten up at all. My brother, Jim, and my sister, Kathie are both older than me and if they were asked, I'm sure they'd tell you that Sally didn't really eat the second dessert every night...that was me also.

Sally and I used food for solace. Food equaled love to me. Food was always honest and never promised things that would never happen and weren't true to begin with. If there was one thing you could count on in life, it was that peanut butter and jelly sandwich was always the same...unless you used strawberry jam instead of grape jelly...then the texture was really different. There was a grocery store down the street from the apartment we lived in and I'd save up my allowance and walk down to the store and buy a chocolate cake. I'd tell myself that it would be a special surprise for my family, but on my way back home, I always found myself sitting in the field across from our apartment complex devouring the cake one handful at a time. The older I got the things I used to medicate my pain were different. Forever searching for something to make myself feel worthy of love and security I tried drugs, cigarettes, sex, shopping, and a myriad of other temporary fixes but the search continued until I had my first child and I met Jesus Christ.

Dad was found in a motel room when the newspapers had piled up outside the door and the cleaning people had grown concerned. He had been dead for five days... cirrhosis of the liver had finally won. I was ten years old at the time and my parents had been "separated" for a number of years. When the news came that he had died I remember feeling guilty. What if I had tried to talk to him and I could have made him see that we all loved him and he needed to stop drinking and then everything would be fine. What power children think they have and

9

what a painful revelation to discover that we have no power at all. My mom was devastated and couldn't seem to stem the continual tears. My young mind could not understand why she was so upset. I thought she hated him since they no longer lived together and for all those years we were told to tell people that our dad worked in another country and that's why no one ever saw him. As an electrical engineer he did work in Greenland for a time, but I came to realize that that expedition was really a formal separation that no one identified as such. My dad was an abusive alcoholic, but he was also extremely funny when he was sober and could tell stories that would leave you spellbound to the punch line…and there was always a punch line. Dad knew the hardest side of life, yet he continued to see the humor in everyday occurrences and to an extent, I tend to look at life the same way.

Virtually everyone makes their mom out to be the stand in for Mary the mother of Jesus. I've come to understand that my mother and all mothers for that matter do the best they can with what they have to work with. Mom was raised in an affluent home and when she married Dad she took a drastic step to the other side of the tracks. Mom's family was not there to help her when her husband turned out to not be the knight in shining armor she'd dreamed of. Through pure force of will and love for we three kids she carved out a life for us. Mom went to work back when it was not socially acceptable to do so. In my first thirteen years we had moved to twelve different rental homes. I always thought we moved because the next house would be better. I later learned that it was because we were evicted for unpaid rent. What an incredible resourceful woman she was! Mom could make an entire new Easter outfit out of some sheets and a bedspread, dress with matching coat and all. I remember falling asleep to the sound of Mom's sewing machine. She loved us so well that we actually thought she enjoyed staying up all night sewing before going to work without sleep the next day. Oh, the selfishness of childhood. My friend, Sherry, says that you can always count on nothing being thrown out in my home…it always just turns into something else. I've been laughed at for saving tissue paper, boxes, curtains, and what not, but my mom's recycling attitude before it was fashionable has kept my family in times of plenty and in times of want.

After Dad died, Mom instituted a new family plan called "we're a team". Of all the things she imparted to me this concept of family has stuck with me to this day. Back in the day, people would probably have found it comical that we were proud to be a Foy (my maiden name). Somehow my mother was able to make us believe that being a Foy was something really special. Foys were not wimps; they pressed on and never gave up. They stood with other Foys no matter what came their way. A Foy could pick on another Foy, but the Lord help you if you were not one of us and you came against one of us! My girls have known from a very young age that even though they are Leonardellis, they have a large amount of Foy in them and Foy women are strong, faithful, committed women that can do whatever needs to be done no matter the obstacles that seem to be in their way. Foys know in their deepest being that "winners never quit and quitters never win".

Mom died of a cerebral hemorrhage when I was fourteen. Our team was diminished by one, yet for the remaining years, family as a team was our collective strength.

How do you do all things, hard things, painful things through the power of Christ? Oh, the times I've asked myself that same question. It will never cease to amaze me that in whatever circumstances I've found myself I'm never alone. I realize now that minus the standard sinners prayer, I came to know true strength in Christ when I was in labor with Merigen.

Let me preface this by saying that in medicine, there is a general belief that if anything can go wrong in the treatment of a patient, it will occur first to the person who is medical by career choice. If it doesn't affect them, it will find its control over the family members of said medical person. Other than the obvious fact that when your husband is a pediatrician, nurses, lab techs, and other physicians seem to put forth that extra effort. They are also notorious for sharing any unpleasant thing a doctor's family may have experienced. Okay, all medical people reading this are now offended. My friends, if you are honest with yourself you will have to admit that this is in fact, correct. We spend so much time pouring out to others that we secretly hope that the grim aspects of life will affect everyone else…surly not us. And so we talk… hoping that if and when we are singled out as the main topic of conversation, we will be treated with grace.

The other overwhelming challenge is having too much, but not enough knowledge about what is medically affecting us or our loved ones. Haven't you ever wondered why your family practice doctor will send you to an orthopedist when you fracture something? It's because although they have a general idea of what is going on, when they sought to be the best of the best in their specialty they stopped being concerned about how to treat everything under the sun and started to fine tune their knowledge in their area of expertise. Believe me, this is true, other than the physicians with the "God Complex" that think they can do it all. The real Creator of the universe sets them straight. Okay, I get it, you're wondering when I'm going to get to the point.

On the morning of my due date I joked with Phil, my husband, as he was leaving for the hospital to do rounds. "I'll call you when I'm in labor." I said.

"Sure, Babe, you do that," he replied and off to work he went. Twenty minutes later I was on the phone with my sister when I felt a rush of warmth and wetness and I told her that my water had broken. Being ever the skeptic and having had two children of her own by then, Kathie assumed my bladder was over full and the weight of the pregnancy caused an accident. Hanging up quickly, I headed into the bathroom to experience the first wave of fear associated with this delivery. My water did in fact break, but it was meconium stained indicating the baby was in some type of distress. I called Phil first and then my doctor. I was told to take a shower and come in to the doctor's office when I was ready. Phil, of course, was on his way home. Nothing in books or other people's experiences prepares you for the overwhelming fear that something may in fact be wrong with your baby, or God forbid, your baby may die. To this day, twenty nine years later, I can remember the bargaining I did with God while standing in the shower. "Oh God, please, if you exist at all, please don't let anything be wrong with my baby. You wouldn't take all my mistakes out on an innocent baby, would you, God? Please let everything be all right. Please God, my dad died when I was ten and my mom when I was fourteen…please don't take another away from me." The trembling hits you when you can no longer pretend that you aren't in fact scared spitless.

My mind ran pathways I didn't know I had on the way to the doctor's office. I've always had an ability to let the most frightening thing that could happen resolve itself in my heart before anything occurred. That way, I can depend on myself to be calm and levelheaded. Later after whatever is going to happen happens, I can either rejoice that I was so well prepared, or fall completely apart. I think this approach has to do with a childhood of lies and promises not kept. If you don't expect good things to happen, you'll not be disappointed when they don't.

Other than the obvious miracle of childbirth, the most significant thing that happened during labor was the beginning of my search for the Savior. Merigen's heart rate was dropping at times and because I had to be induced, my body wasn't cooperating with the whole laboring process. My true journey toward Christ began when my unborn child was in distress and I put conviction behind my bargaining. "Okay God, if you exist and you care even a little bit about me, please don't let my baby die…If you're there, I need this baby, Lord…it's the start of the family I always wanted. If this baby is okay, I'll find you and serve you and do whatever you want me to do from now on. I promise God, I know I usually lie to get my way, but this time God, I am so really serious. Amen or whatever." Twenty one hours after my water broke Merigen Jo Leonardelli was born. She was in perfect health and I had a promise to keep.

"Behold how good and how pleasant it is, for brethren to dwell together in unity!"

~ Psalm 133:1 ~
ASV

I was raised in the Catholic Church and although I walked away after my mother died when I was fourteen, the lessons learned burn deep within. Feeling responsible for the faith and "acceptability" of my daughter in the eyes of God, I discussed returning to the only faith Phil and I had known. Funny how when you're just worrying about you, you'll play Russian roulette with God, but when you are responsible for someone else's relationship with God your actions are more calculated. Wow! That'll preach!... We began discussions of life, death, and everything in between and I know now that God was preparing us for the invitation that would change our lives forever.

Phil is a Pediatrician and at that time he was doing a lot of intensive care nursery duty in addition to his medical practice. That left me home alone with the baby a fair amount of the time. Back before the vastness of program choices, we were living in Great Falls, Montana, population 60,000, and we had five local television stations. There was a very small two pound infant just born that needed to be transported to a larger city for care and Phil would once again be home very late. I started to channel surf through the whole five channels and lo and behold, the choices were a gardening show on one channel and the Billy Graham Crusade on the other four. I uttered some expletives about how the religious crazies were forcing their paranoid garbage on to the rest of us sane people and how I would be writing a letter of complaint to those four stations, oh just you wait and see...they'd be sorry after they heard from me. Preparing to turn the TV off, I moved toward the off switch (no remotes then) and something deep inside me (akin to the

16

"heads up" feeling I spoke of previously) told me to wait and listen.

The following is not a direct quote from Billy Graham, but the meaning, I believe, is the same. He said something like this...

"Is your life void of true meaning? Are you lonely, needing peace, and an outlet for the pain that life has dealt you? Maybe you've been abandoned by those you love...I'm here to tell you there is a Savior who knows exactly how you feel. He was wounded for every sin you will ever commit, he was crucified for all the pain, hurt, and heartache this world has to offer and He alone can bring you the peace and love that you so desire. If you are ready to admit that you are a sinner, your way has not worked and you need a Savior, then you need Jesus Christ. Make your way from all over the auditorium down to the front. There are people here ready to pray with you and bring you to the place of peace you've longed for." Wait a minute; did he say peace and acceptance? Is that what I've been missing? What do you have to do to get it? "For those of you at home, you know the Lord Jesus is calling you to Him. What you can do on your own will never fill the hole inside of you, only Jesus can do that. As people from all over are answering the call of God to repent and accept the Savior, you at home do the same." Okay wait a minute...Mom and Dad are dead, is this the family I'm looking for? All those people going forward look like nice enough people. What would it be like to have friends and family that do the right thing...the things God wants for us? Oh great. I missed that, what was I supposed to pray to make this work? I only caught the tail end of the prayer, but it was enough to repeat that I wanted

Jesus to be my Lord and Savior and to send for the free information to the address on the screen.

When Phil came home later that night, I told him what had happened and being the intelligent man that he is, he agreed that we should look over the information when it came and see what we should do after that. My birth into Christ came as a result of that information and our lives from the moment of the prayer of repentance and salvation would never be the same. Little did I know then that although the walk with Jesus would always be worth it, the price to pay for the free gift can be mighty.

Our oldest kids, Jenny and David, were being raised Catholic by their mom and stepdad and we naturally assumed that returning to the Catholic tradition was the right thing to do. We called the priest that ministered on the campus of a small college in our town and set up a meeting with him. Why a meeting, you may ask?...simply because we had both been taught a reverence for the church even though we lived a life that didn't embrace it, if you're smart, you don't defile the house of God without a confession of who and what you really are.

Father Steve was an awesome example of true Christian love. He was young, athletic, and enthused about bringing the simple faith in the Gospel to the people of God. We made a plan to begin taking classes in the faith to refresh and in some cases correct our understanding of the faith. After completion of the classes, we renewed our vows and had Merigen baptized in the church.

My husband is a sponge in that new occurrences and new information in his life are to be thoroughly investigated. From the "Amen" of his salvation, he had a passion for reading the Bible. He threw out anything that did not honor God in his life and he made church and prayer a top priority. Me…I was not so fired up about the whole lifestyle change. I could see where going to strip clubs, reading porn, and getting drunk should probably be stopped, but the constant Bible reading? Give me a break. However, wanting to be the perfect wife, I began to read the Bible daily. The problem was that I started with Genesis and I read right before bed. Consequently I had nightmares most nights and a deep seated fear that God was going to wipe me off the face of the earth any minute. Hey! This was not the love and acceptance that I thought it was going to be!

We had returned to the Catholic Church and began to listen with new insight. So much of the meaning of the mass is lost in rote tradition. We would make the sign of the cross at the correct time, kneel, stand, pray the same prayers, but anything done repetitiously will eventually be done without thought. The personal Jesus that I had so hoped to meet had not knocked on the door of my heart as yet and I needed something to teach me freedom in faith.

Good friends of ours had been trying to get us to join them at their non denominational church for a few months. Looking for something more, we joined them one Sunday and found what we thought this family of God was supposed to be. The people were so warm and inviting. The worship music was awesome and Phil, being a guitar player, was instantly intrigued with this form of music. We made good friends there, these were the kinds of friends that watch each other's kids and have barbeques. We went on camping trips with our home fellowship group and truly felt that this was what God invited us to.

As we became more involved I started to notice how impressed the ministry staff was with "Doctor Leonardelli". At the same time it was apparent that only some folks in the body should have an opinion and the rest should just be good quiet little worker bees. Wait a minute...hold up...I thought it said in the book of James that we weren't supposed to prefer people because of wealth, or position! Hmmm. I guess the family of God is just like everyone else deep down. Of all the lessons I've learned, or am learning, this has been the hardest for me. People come to Christ, but they are still people and no matter how much we'd like to deny it, some are more worthy in our own eyes than others. Thank God that He doesn't think as we do, or Heaven would be a pretty empty place. Unknowingly, we in that fellowship set a standard that all who wanted to belong should measure up to. We were seemingly sinless, beautiful people. We wore stylish clothes, had clean cars, nice homes, and closet sin. I hid the fact that I was a smoker for years when I realized that, according to some preset standard, I should have reached perfection already. The church we belonged to was Charismatic and moved in the gifts of the Spirit. I remember being terrified that at some point, a prophetic utterance would come forth that would expose who I really was. To this day, when I bring forth an altar call in the church that I pastor, my heart breaks for those that are afraid to come forward and let the truth of their struggles be known. What have we done to the church today when we preach God's unmerited favor and send a message of unacceptability to those that hunger for grace while feeling judged? What have we done to the pastorate that men and women who love God fall away to adultery, thievery, and all other forms of sin while our church councils sit by saying in essence, "thank God that the poor guy, or gal wasn't in our church! We should have a message done on the perils of falling away." Wait a minute, maybe the person didn't fall away. Maybe we set a judgmental standard so high that they were afraid to be honest and get help or support. Is it just me, or are the standards losing sight of the grace? I've experienced the "lynch mob" and when people treat you like you have a contagious disease; you have few to discuss your life with other than your family and the Lord. As the psalmist says "How good it is to dwell together in unity"! Okay, so we missed the meaning behind that one.

I don't understand to this day what it's all about. How incredibly shallow people's lives must be that they need to tear down what God is trying to do in order to build themselves up. From my personal experience in ministry my heart breaks for those that are caught up in the pettiness of a lie. Some will go on to serve the Lord, but some will walk completely away. After all, why be part of a church that eats its own? If we want to feel like garbage, we can just hang out in the world. Isn't that why Christians are often called hypocrites? I received an apology letter from a friend, who at one time years ago, was part of a "lynch mob" that formed against me in my church. How I praise God for that apology, not because she admitted she was wrong, but because it affirmed for me that my broken heart mattered to God. It amazes me that in the midst of my deepest hurts, or darkest fears, I always forget how God brought me through in the past.

Maybe the greatest gift we could give to new believers is the insight to remember. Write it down and create your own memorial journal. Then when you wonder why you're doing this thing called "Christianity", you'll recall how it was before you made your choice.

One event that will forever be on the journal of my heart is the gift of our adopted daughter, Kalie Shae Leonardelli.

"But in my distress I cried out to the Lord; yes, I prayed to my God for help. He heard me from His sanctuary; my cry reached His ears."

~ Psalm 18:6 ~
NLT

Few people can understand the pain associated with infertility. There is that seed of desire in every couple that wants to see what kind of person their love will produce. Will he have your eyes, or my nose? Will she have small feet, or chunky toes? Hey…not bad for a rhyme! What a vast array of emotion is associated with the God given desire to "be fruitful and multiply". The afternoon of Merigen's birth, I had a scheduled tubal ligation. Phil and I had our family planned out. Jenny was five and David was three, making our blended family perfect in stair steps. Our problem was the same as so many before and after us. We made a plan prior to giving our lives to Christ and after, we wondered if somehow we had messed up God's plan for our family. Thanks to modern medicine, we had an opportunity to reverse our decision with a very expensive, four hour laser surgery and when Merigen was two, that's what we did.

The following six months were a series of temperature taking every morning, timed intimacy, fertility drugs, and shattered dreams every month that went by without a pregnancy. And then, the blessing we had prayed for…I was pregnant. I naturally assumed that since this miracle had taken so long to achieve, God would bless us with a healthy baby eight months from then. Not a stop at the store could occur without going to check out maternity clothes. If I found something I couldn't live without, I'd buy it and tell myself that I'd need it soon anyway. By three months into the pregnancy I was wearing maternity clothes. Shortly before four months I felt the fluttering of our baby as he grew and stretched and matured for life outside the womb. The kids and I would talk to him and make plans for him. Merigen was really excited because when Jenny and David went home to their mom and stepdad's, she would no longer be alone. We called the baby "him" because in our young faith, we approached God like the "Santa Claus in the sky" and since we already had two girls, obviously He could see that we needed another boy to balance out the perfect family unit. You see, we had done what we saw as our part in this bargain with God. We read our Bibles, attended church three times a week, and prayed daily. Why would God not bless us with what we asked for? Isn't that how it works?

Our first lesson in God is God and I am not, came when I was four months pregnant.

I stood in front of my closet trying to decide what shirt to wear. I don't remember why it mattered, except I know I had some place I was supposed to be. Yellow has always seemed to me to be a promising color…you know, like black is elegant, or sad, depending on your mood and red says "HERE I AM!" Yellow is a color of promise and I was so filled with joy over my little girl, my husband, my step kids and the baby we would all one day enjoy, that nothing could possibly dampen my mood. I was all ready to go when I decided to make one more stop in the bathroom before leaving the house.

There are a myriad of feeling words that authors have used to describe an event that changes the life of an individual. When I looked down and realized that I was bleeding my feelings went first to absolute unbelief. "Oh no, this can't be happening to me. God wouldn't answer my prayer just to take it away. This can't be a miscarriage." My thoughts spun out of control and then went to numb silence. I cleaned myself up and stood in front of the toilet looking at the water. Ridiculous as it may sound,

I truly had to consider if I should flush the toilet or not, because I might be flushing away my child, my hope, and my belief system. Years of habit led me to "not forget to flush" and I walked very slowly and carefully downstairs to the living room. It sounds crazy but I really thought that if I could be gentle enough, my baby would be fine.

I lay down on the couch and elevated my legs hoping that gravity would keep the baby inside. Mental check lists ran through my mind...

"Do I have any pain?" I asked myself.

"No", I replied.

"Any cramping at all?" I further questioned myself.

"No, I'm really feeling just fine...well, other than the cold blooded fear that my baby is dying inside me while I lay here and do nothing!" I answered myself.

"Do you think you should call Phil and let him know what's going on?" I asked myself.

"Well, you know I probably should...but that will make this nightmare real. Don't you think I should lay here for a little while longer and pretend nothing is wrong?" I questioned.

"Okay", I replied, "no sense in shattering a dream unless I absolutely have to."

"When will I know that it's time to call Phil?" I asked myself.

"When the numbness is complete and I can say that I think the baby is dead without screaming and pulling my hair out. Then I can call Phil."

The problem was that the only way I knew I could maintain my sanity was with Phil by my side and so, I called him.

My husband is a "knight in shining armor" kind of

guy. If a problem is presented to him or a concern is voiced, Phil will respond with some type of solution. When I told him I was bleeding he first assured me that lots of women have that occur and the baby is fine, and then he told me to call my OB Doctor.

Somewhere inside of me is the ability based on need, to have everything "under control" at all times. As I was speaking to my doctors' nurse, I sounded like I was reciting the weather...partly cloudy with the chance of a full nervous breakdown. I was told to go in to his office and they'd see what was going on. My heart wanted to believe that this was nothing serious, but my head knew I was losing our baby. Oh what bliss it is when we can tell ourselves that the world is not ending while the bombs go off all around us.

After seeing my doctor so he could confirm that I was not in fact, exaggerating, and I was losing a significant amount of blood, I went to X-ray for an ultrasound. People are abnormally quiet when they think that tragedy has struck. If sound waves are too vibrant, the tiny threadlike faith that holds us together may fracture.

The ultrasound tech moves the wand over my skin stopping to record pictures of the contents of my uterus. But no tiny baby lives there anymore and no amount of silence or polite clearing of the throat can assuage my personal hell at that moment in time. All medical personnel should go through some kind of course that teaches warm comments for the worse times in people's lives. A word to all of you who haven't taken the course... DO NOT tell the patient that you don't know but the doctor will contact you sometime before the millennial reign of Christ. Trust me, it's not helpful.

My faith was rocked to its core by the miscarriage of our baby. Those who have experienced this horror will agree with me that although well meaning people tell you things like, "at least it wasn't a real baby", or "you think you've had it bad! My sister's friend's cousin had a miscarriage when she was a full month further along than you! What do you think of that?"

Truthfully, I think that sucks. And I'm grieving my lost child. You see...this baby was as real to me as my other kids and no other person, or child will take that special baby's place. Dreams and promises are not replicable and as I screamed and cried out to God for an answer, I learned that God truly can do whatever He wants. I also learned that love is as deep and as vast as the seas and the love a parent has for a child is unending. And finally I learned that I have the ability and desire to love any child who needs a mom.

God my Father had promised me another child and she came through the gift of adoption by a brave and loving teenage mom.

It was the beginning of summer and Phil, Merigen and I packed up the car for a road trip from Durango, Colorado where we lived to Great Falls, Montana where Jenny and David lived. We were picking up the kids to drive back to Durango for "our part" of the summer. While we were there we'd stay with my sister, Kathie and her two kids, Lloyd and Ginger. One of the things we looked forward to was returning to the church that had first raised us in the knowledge of Jesus Christ.

On Sunday we were greeting people in the lobby when a dear friend of mine told me that her daughter was pregnant and was planning to choose a family to adopt her baby.

It was as though the Holy Spirit himself was talking to me and I knew that her daughter's baby was the child that God meant for us to have.

"Every good and every perfect gift comes down from the Father of Heavenly lights, with which there is no variation or shadow of turning."

~ James 1:17 ~
NKJV

Cookie Leonardelli

A sense of profound peace entered my heart and I knew beyond any reason that God wanted this baby to be ours. "We'll adopt the baby." I heard tumbling from my mouth. What am I saying, I questioned myself. I haven't even mentioned this to Phil...shouldn't I run this life altering decision by him?

My dear friend looked so relieved that I knew I'd heard God in this. Service was about to start so I told her we'd talk after and made my way to the seat Phil had saved for me.

"What?" He asked, sensing that there was something I needed to tell him. The music began for the first worship song and I replied, "Nothing". Nothing! What was I thinking? That wasn't just a lie; it was a denial of the life altering change that I knew would be part of our lives. But how exactly do you tell the love of your life that you've committed him to a lengthily legal, emotional, financial, heart wrenching rollercoaster that has no absolute guarantee of success, in order to fulfill the need you have to mother just one more child? Only a man in tune with our great big God could possibly agree to this.

Somewhere in the middle of the worship, while Phil had his hands raised in surrender to the God he serves; I elbowed him in the ribs. So much for respecting his time in the throne room of God! "Lucy's (fictitious name) daughter is pregnant and wants the baby to be adopted so I told her we'd adopt the baby." Seems like there should be a smiley face in response to that declaration, but as Phil's arms returned to his sides, he looked at me with such shock that I was almost speechless (for those that know me speechlessness is not one of my attributes). "What?" I asked.

"Babe," he whispered, "this is one of those things we should have prayed about or at least discussed before we committed to it!"

"I know, but I'm really sure that this is what God wants us to do! It is probably the reason I lost the baby, and why we came to this service, and Lucy seemed so relieved..." I tend to ramble when I need to justify something that I've said or done. By now the people around us were clearly annoyed by our whispered conversation so we resumed singing and waited to discuss the adoption until after the service. Maybe I should say Phil resumed singing. I was lost in the world of contentment that in no time at all, I'd be holding a new baby in my arms. Oh the wonder of God's creations! A complete package of potential just waiting to develop into all God intends. How excited Merigen, Jenny, and David would be! David would want a boy for sure, but Merigen would just be pleased to have a sibling that always stayed at our house. Oh yes, I told myself, this is absolutely perfect.

Kalie's birth mom came to live with us for the last month of her pregnancy, and we were there when Kalie was born. What a wonderful and horrible experience that was! For our family to be so profoundly blessed, her birth mom had to experience the tearing away of the child that had been part of her for nine months. I have nothing but deep admiration for any birthparents that love their babies so much that they put the baby's need above their own and choose parents to raise their child. The respect that I have for Kalie's birth mom is as fierce as my love for Kalie.

Her adoption was finalized when she was a year old. A year that had us living in fear that somehow, someway her birth family would take her back and we'd be the ones feeling the deep tearing and the huge void. God was truly my refuge and strength during that time and as I prayed for our family, I prayed for Kalie's birth family as well. After all, we are all related in the family of God. I also learned a lot about myself in that process.

I came to realize that I am completely able to love all my children with a fierce mother love. Two are step kids, one is birth, and one is adopted, but all are part of me and through the next years I came to understand that in ways I never dreamed were even possible.

Mother love can be as irrational as Father love and protection can be. When someone picked on one of my kids, I automatically assumed it was the other kids fault. My kids would never be hurtful or cause harm to another child! Ok, there was Jenny's first day of kindergarten when she and some little friends pushed a little kid down and took his backpack from him. I'll never forget Phil's face when his ex wife called to tell him what Jenny had done. "No way would Jenny do that!" He yelled, "Are they trying to set her up or something?....What? There were witnesses...but why would she do such a thing?" The passion with which he defended Jenny gave way to sadness that I hadn't seen before. There was such disappointment in his body language and face that my heart broke for Phil. Having worked in a childcare center I knew that even though we'd like to believe that our kids will always stand up for the underdog, more often than not, they are just rejoicing that they are the torturer and not the tortured.

Isn't that the way with most people? We witness horrific events and thank God that it was someone else's child, or family, or marriage. To be open to others pain causes more compassion to rise up in our hearts and minds, but it also makes us vulnerable and somewhat afraid that the next time, it could be me that suffers the tragedy. I think that's why some of us even as adults are afraid to step on a crack...What if it really does break your mothers back?

I know of course that it doesn't, but we as people are always searching for the way to make our lives sadness proof. If we pray enough, do enough good deeds, help the down trodden, then peril and pain will avoid us...or so we hope. Yet I've lived through some things that only my love and faith in God have gotten me through and some of the things that I've learned by standing strong have given me the ability to help when others are in pain.

Fast forward several years and our family was doing well by most standards. Merigen was in a private school as a freshman, and on drill team. Kalie was also in private school, second grade, and in dance (although she was very much the tom boy). And for the first time in eighteen years, Jenny had moved in with us, attended a year of college, and took the summer and what was to be a year off of school, to work at Lone Tree Bible Ranch. David visited that summer and returned to Montana for his senior year of high school.

Jenny was in her element. The atmosphere is peaceful and life changing at Lone Tree. She made some close friends on staff, learned to be a repelling instructor, and fell in love with God and a young man. She came home for a few weekends that summer always bringing friends and I think that Merigen and Kalie missed her attention, but they learned as all siblings do, that everybody grows up and their lives change. It's the way growing up is intended to be. You grow up and then before you know it, you're out on your own. Still, the fact that Jenny was the only one excited when Kalie brought a gold fish home from the fair, made her very significant in Kalie's life. (In my defense I had told her NOT to bring home a goldfish!)

Merigen missed the alone time with Jenny since they shared a room, secrets, and life plans. And David had leaned on and been supported by Jenny his entire life so her growing away from him in some ways was bittersweet.

If only we'd learn to truly love and appreciate the people in our lives and to be sure to tell them how we feel. Then every night before we are enveloped in sleep, we'd know that we'd done our very best on that day.

Thank God for strong hugs and last minute "I love yous".

"God grant me the serenity
to accept the things I cannot change,
The courage to change the things I can,
And the wisdom to know the difference.
Living one day at a time,
enjoying one moment at a time;
Accepting hardship as a pathway to peace;
Taking as Jesus did,
this sinful world as it is,
not as I would have it,
Trusting that You will make all things right
if I surrender to your will;
So that I may be reasonably happy
in this life and supremely happy with you
forever in the next."
Amen

~ Reinhold Niebuhr ~

We fear losing the image we've created, and so we plaster the walls of our lives with pictures meant to preserve. The memories though, become as lies when the world continues to age and the child likeness in the picture never does.

I've attempted conversation about how things were, yet many avert their eyes, or cough self consciously into the back of their hand. We mustn't talk I suppose, because the pain so effectively suffocated for so long will boil up and become...become what? The fear of every mother stands as a wall between me and all who were once comfortable in my company.

The sights and smells and sounds are clear to this day. There are everyday feelings that we all take for granted. The noise of the cars outside, the hum of the heat vents, the smell of coffee left over from the morning...and yet the rain grows louder and the friendly washing of the earth becomes somehow menacing.

Memories are often more real than the experience.

Merigen was running late as was often the case. To say she had an active life would be an understatement. At fourteen she possessed the promise of the beautiful woman she'd one day be. She torpedoed into the kitchen for help with the back buttons on her drill team uniform, tying her shoes as she hopped toward me.

"Are you sure you have to go to be a support to the soccer team? It's been raining since last night and the field is probably flooded." I hoped we'd be able to pass on this outing. Driving the forty minutes to school with flooded arroyos was not my idea of good Saturday fun. "Maybe you should call the coach to be sure."

"Mom, you know that even if they cancel the game,

they'll expect us to show up just to prove that we would have been there to support the soccer team. NO excuses, was all we heard during the entire practice yesterday! I have to go even if we need a boat to get there!" she answered. The fine lines and small dark shadows of fatigue turned Mer's face into that of a wizened, yet exhausted, child. This drill team schedule is ridiculous, I silently fumed. If they aren't at practice, they're being support to all the other teams. Whatever happened to free time to just hang out in your pajamas all day, I wondered.

"Anyway," Mer sighed, "I'm ready". Heading for the front door, she yelled her good-byes to Phil and I attempted to persuade Kalie, then eight, to join me for yet another trip down to Merigen's school.

"I think cars make me sick when I'm not going anywhere good," Kalie moaned.

"Where's good?" I asked.

"A pizza place, a toy store, stuff like that," she responded.

Finding it impossible to argue with such sound reasoning, I accepted the fact that enjoying Kalie's company for the drive was not going to be my pleasure today. Grabbing my purse and car keys, I turned to leave when the phone rang. Reaching for the receiver, I had no way of knowing that the conversation I was about to have would change me, challenge my faith, and test me in ways no other call could. The impact of the call would resonate through the rest of my life and the lives of my husband, our kids, our friends, and our church.

Exasperated at the delay, I answered abruptly (so

the caller would know I was feeling intruded upon), "Hello".

"Is this Cookie…Jenny's Mom?" a female voice inquired. Most people that know our family call me stepmom, so I was instantly on alert.

"Yes, this is Cookie, what can I do for you…I'm really in a hurry", I replied.

"I work with Jen at the Italian restaurant in Capitan. She was supposed to work today, but no one has heard from her and she didn't come in for her shift. Is she there?"

There are moments in life when your heart starts beating rapidly and your head asks, why, but you know something is definitely wrong. "Maybe she's at Lone Tree Ranch. Did you try there?" I asked. Why are my palms sweating I asked myself. Merigen had been pacing by the door but now she stood stock still staring at me, trying to figure out what this conversation was about.

"No, nobody has seen her since she left work here last night about nine. It was raining pretty hard and I tried to talk her into staying until it passed, but she was heading back to Lone Tree to make brownies. She wanted to visit with a friend from down your way that was up here for the weekend." Her voice had an edge of panic rising from what began as misunderstanding and concern. "Where could she be? Are you sure she's not with you? I guess she really is missing."

"Explain missing, are you serious?" I responded, "Are you saying that you really have no idea where she is! Has anyone seen her car?"

"I'm sorry that I've upset you, she probably is with

her boyfriend, right?" This woman was trying so hard to sound unconcerned that her voice held a slight echo.

Jenny's boyfriend had gone back home to Texas for a week or so; that being the case and knowing Jenny to be ultra responsible, I knew that something was very wrong. "I'll see what I can find out, "I said, "Thank you so much for calling. Please let me know if you hear from her."

After promising to stay in touch if either of us heard from her, I hung up the phone to call Lone Tree. Merigen continued to stare at me and ask what was going on and I told her that her sister was missing and I was calling Lone Tree. They told me that a search party had gone out in the surrounding area and that going was slow because there had been a flash flood out of the mountains the night before. Some said it moved about fifty-five miles per hour, and it took trees, bikes, tires, and anything that was in its path in the direction of the dam. The tiny stream that runs across the road to Lone Tree Ranch became a violent river. And so far, there was no trace of Jenny or her car. "Should we come and help with the search?" I asked. Obviously there is an appropriate way to deal with a missing child but for the life of me, I couldn't figure it out.

"No, it's better for you to stay there in case she gets in touch with you," was the reply. The Ranch would stay in touch with me and I'd stay in touch with them and surly we'd find her. I kept thinking that maybe she got out of her car and a branch knocked her out…She could be wandering around wondering where she was…maybe she'd been abducted! Oh please God, no, don't let her be hurt! Prayers flow through panic faster than salt through a shaker.

I called for Phil and Kalie so they could hear the news, and told Merigen to call her coach because she was definitely not going to the game, and I started calling people that I knew would pray.

*"For everything there is a season,
A time for every activity
under heaven."*

~ Ecclesiastes 3:1 ~
NLT

I married Phil when I was twenty-five. He was a Pediatrician in private practice in Great Falls, Montana. His prior marriage had left him with many wonderful memories, but the tangible proof of a love that had been blessed were found in the personalities of Jenny, then three and a half, and David, eighteen months.

When I first met Jenny the word that imprinted on my mind was intense. She had long dark blonde hair and crystal blue eyes that were shadowed by a shelf of bangs covering her forehead. Her questions were unending, her opinion readily expressed (though never researched), and the responsibility she felt for her younger brother was never more evident than when she corralled him along...much like a sheepdog. Full of wide eyed wonder, she loved to create make believe stories and could often be discovered talking to herself about "stuff". A writer, I thought, and I hoped to one day share in that creativity.

David was the family absorber. He tended to quietly take in the activity that surrounded him as though he were photographing the moment behind his toddler eyes. His hair was so blonde and his eyes so blue that, similar to a masters painting, you felt them penetrating your core when he glanced your way. David was as pensive as Jenny was intense. A reluctant follower, he tagged along simply because that was what was expected of him. While Jenny would plow ahead like a demolition crew seeking the end result, David would wait, hoping that his need, desire, or interest would come to him.

I remember him sitting at the shore of a lake on a family camping trip, right at the edge where the water is a couple of inches deep and it gently laps at your legs. He'd been watching the water for awhile with the concentration that some use with video games. I approached him slowly hoping to catch a glimpse of what had so completely captivated his interest. He'd reach into the water, pull back his hand, slowly open his chubby fingers and frown as he observed his wet, empty palm. It took me a few minutes to realize that he was trying to catch a tadpole. He continued "fishing" for another half hour or so until he finally made contact. The look of pure delight as he opened his hand and observed the tiny creature was indescribable. As he attempted to put the tadpole in his mouth, it fell from his slippery hand as was freed to swim away. What could a toddler possibly need such patience and perseverance for, I wondered, as I watched him begin his quest anew.

Although Jenny and David lived primarily with their mom and stepdad, they were just eight blocks away in the early years of our marriage. We saw them on the agreed upon schedule and looked forward to them being the older siblings to Merigen, born a couple of years after we were married.

"Tunie", as we called her, was the actress, dancer, performing artist among the three. Always wanting to play pretend, she'd cast herself in the role of the princess and delegate supporting roles to her sister and brother. A bedspread became a castle when hung from the posts of her bed...a cardboard box, her throne, as she held court in the middle of her bedroom. At two, she had a halo of auburn wavy hair and golden green eyes that lit with excitement when a new audience for her performances entered the room.

The performer, the director that the world saw often masked the deeply sensitive and loyal little girl that made

Merigen who she really was and who she continues to be. She took the separations from Jenny and David hard and seemed to store lists of things to do when they were all together again.

The unity that existed between our three children was not, I've come to believe, typical of half siblings, yet the essence of family that made them one was more a unity of spirit than of blood. Never was this more evident than when we adopted Kalie. Jenny was eleven, David was nine, and Merigen was six when their collective prayers were answered in the birth of our youngest.

Kalie was born with dark brown hair and eyes that possessed the fierce determination to be heard above all else. She was, and still is, and explorer. Boundaries didn't exist in Kalie's world. All authority was to be questioned even in matters such as, why we should eat green beans when applesauce tastes so much better? When Kalie passed her first birthday, we were finally able to complete her adoption. It was the longest year of my life. Waiting and praying that nothing would go wrong and that this beautiful baby would forever be part of our family was my constant companion. Within a month of her finalization, Kalie's hair turned blonde and her eyes blue, exactly like David's. She truly became a Leonardelli not just in name, but in appearance as well. Even today, people think she's joking when she says she's adopted.

Kalie has a propensity to be drawn to the underdog. It started with anything furry and progressed to reptiles, snakes, and even people. For a long time we were bombarded with an array of creatures that our miniature Dr. Doolittle brought home. We've had cats, guinea pigs, dogs, snails, hamsters and for a year we even leased a horse. Anything she tried athletically, she mastered like a natural. Dancing came as easily to her as walking, but Kalie is best expressed by her sense of humor and her smile.

Merigen was fourteen, David was seventeen and Kalie was eight when our world was turned upside down with the news that Jenny's body had been found.

They determined that she was most likely attempting to gage whether or not she could cross the stream on the way back to Lone Tree Ranch. She probably got out of her car to check the depth when the wall of water came storming down the creek. Her car was found a couple of miles from where she had gotten out. Twenty-four hours later, her body was found face down in a field near the dam. She had a few small scratches, but was otherwise unharmed…her shoes were still tied.

I choose to believe that an angel picked her up and deposited her safely in the field. To think that God would call her back to Himself without protecting her journey is unfathomable to me.

She'd permed her hair just a week before she died. Jenny and her boyfriend had been home briefly just last week. When she left I hugged her and told her to be safe. No one else was home and later Mer would comment that she wished she'd been able to hug Jenny one more time. I wonder, if we knew our conversations with others were to be our last, would they hold more love? Are there any words for our kids other than, "Oh, I love you so much… please be happy, safe, content…please feel my deep love for you. My baby, my toddler, and now my journeying teen. Please don't go so far away from me that you lose your way home." But she didn't choose to lose her way, and in fact she didn't lose her way. No, my oldest child gifted to me in my marriage forged the path to Father God like all those who have passed away before her. It's because Jesus was Jenny's Lord and Savior that we know we'll see her again.

Peace can be found in horrible situations if we will only remember that this life is but a moment in eternity. But oh, the searing pain that hits when you realize that there is absolutely nothing that you can do to remove yourself from the circumstances you are forced to face. I believe that all of our experiences prepare us for the issues and trials that will follow in our life. Many will say that to lose a child is the worst thing anyone could ever go through. I've come to realize that all people have experiences that for them are even worse. After all, we know where Jenny is. How horrible for those whose child is simply missing.

I guess it all depends on your perspective...but at the time, hell is still hell.

When Jenny was missing, life stopped. I felt guilty if I fell asleep as though my vigil would somehow assure a good outcome. The first night she was not found, I lay in bed for hours replaying pictures from her life. I prayed for our family and for her mom and stepdad. I begged God and bargained with God and at some point fell asleep. When I awoke in the morning there was a blissful few seconds before I was jolted by the realization that Jenny was missing.

In waiting mode time does weird things. You think hours have passed and it's only been minutes, or minutes have passed but it has really been hours. Eventually you just want an answer. If she won't be found, you want to know. If she's dead, you want to know. Something, anything is better than not knowing. The phone rings and your heart stops. Is this the call you've been hoping for yet dreading? When you discover that it's a telemarketer, your words are harsh and cruel. After all, how could they call when your child is missing?

When the call came that told us her car had been discovered front down in the creek, driver's door open, and her body was not in it, we allowed ourselves to believe that somehow, she'd made it. Somewhere in the surrounding landscape we believed she waited for rescue. Maybe she'd be dazed, maybe she'd have amnesia, but we'd get her back to wholeness together, we were a team. The call that I was sure would bring good news came; only the news wasn't what we'd hoped for.

I can see myself clearly answering the phone. I was completely still as I listened and remained calm and felt somewhat detached. All hope, all strength left me yet my consuming thought was, "Oh God, how do I tell everyone when there is no way to fix this? What do I say to Phil? How do I call her mom and give her this news?" I thanked the caller, hung up the phone, and told those that were waiting that they'd found her, but she didn't make it. Even as my mouth formed the words, my mind wasn't grasping the impact. Having served God for years and knowing that His plan for us is the best plan, I could not wrap my mind around the fact that we were being called by God to suffer this enormous pain.

Ridiculous thoughts ran through my mind. "What should we do with Jenny's Christmas stocking? Do we hang it in memory, or just ignore the fact that the six of us is now five? What do I do with her things? We'll have

49

to go to the Ranch and pack her stuff up. Jenny doesn't live there anymore...not here either and not in Montana. No, Jenny is with God and now those of us that love her get to figure out how to go forward without the fear that if this could happen to us, what else will be allowed in our family?" Once you experience tragedy, you somehow feel like that was your life share and now you'll be done, but I discovered that again, one issue prepares you for the next. I've come to believe that the multitude of tasks that need to be attended to after a loved one dies are the very things that keep you sane and focused while the pain is so new. Later, when the family and friends return to their lives and you are left alone with your thoughts, the need for a shoulder to cry on becomes greatest.

Jesus said, "Come to me all of you who are weary and carry heavy burdens, and I will give you rest. Take my yoke upon you. Let me teach you, because I am humble and gentle of heart, and you will find rest for your souls."

~ Matthew 11:28-29 ~
NLT

They came like a small army, these women, arms burdened with food…hearts burdened with fear and a tinge of guilt. Guilt seems like an inappropriate term for those tending to the grief stricken. Yet who among us when dealt the worse possible could say other than, "thank God it wasn't my child." We pacify ourselves with sentiments such as, "they're much stronger than us, they'll handle this alright", and the tried and true statement spoken as a balm that some people of faith try to apply, "it's God's will." Please tell me why we assume that stating the obvious, i.e. the events of life being God's will (of course life and death are in His hands), how is that supposed to take away the devastation?

I feel no anger or malice toward these women. They're my friends. They've become my lifeline now and will see me through the minutes, days, and months ahead until I am able to breathe again without the catch in my throat or the now familiar shudder.

Why do we reach for food, we women, when life throws us a curve ball? When Jenny, David, Merigen, or Kalie got a bad grade, had a fight with a friend, or wrestled with an issue of life we broke out the ice cream. In lieu of that working, we broke out the always works Leonardelli cure; we made spaghetti. Bagels and cakes, casseroles and salads, lunchmeat and cheese mingled with unshed tears.

Your daughter is dead. Here, eat this bagel. But no one has been able to tell me how to melt the lump in my throat in order to even consider swallowing the bagel that everyone seems to think will erase my pain. How do I get past the primal scream lodged deep in my stomach afraid to dislodge it for fear that the scream, the horror of what we're living through will never end? My thoughts bombarded me, memories flash across my field of vision even with my eyes open. She's three and she's dancing in the living room. She's waiting for Daddy to come home from the office. She's playing bride with Merigen. Jenny was the one that told Kalie "good job" when she won the goldfish at the fair. She was thrilled to be chosen to work at Lone Tree for the summer. She had fallen in love and wanted her mom and stepdad to meet the guy. Jenny was going to be a writer, a wife, a mother. She was protected by God when a lightning storm struck when she was on a mountain top just one week before and she told us that her hair literally stood on end. And now she's gone and with her passing goes all the hopes and dreams all of us had with her for her life here on earth.

There are moments in life that define your direction from then on. Finally alone in the house, I paced without plan. How do I survive this pain? When the one thing you never dreamed would happen happens…what do you do? The sobs welled up from deep inside and I cried out to Jesus like I never had before and I gave him a challenge… "Lord, I can't do this! You will have to help me live through this or I won't make it! Help me." And a peace that I'd never known passed through me and hasn't left. All I am and all I will ever be are because of the loving hand of Jesus Christ.

At the memorial service a friend came up to me and pleaded with me not to leave God because of Jenny's death. That statement has resounded through my heart all these years since and I still don't get how or why anyone would leave the loving arms of God when He's the only one that can bring peace and sanity to pain. When God's son, Jesus, died on the cross for the sins of mankind, He felt grief too. And I was never left alone. Phil, David, Merigen, Kalie and Jen and David's mom and stepdad were walking this road with me. And never forget all my "have a bagel sisters"! They brought solace along with food.

After all, when the cupboards are full, how can life slam to a stop?

"You can please some of the people some of the time..."

~ Abraham Lincoln ~

I'm not sure exactly how you maneuver the curve balls of life. Just when you think you've got this thing handled, some occurrence or some person proves to you that you don't have it at all.

At the time of Jenny's death I was a leader in our kids club at church. It was called the "Good News Bears" club and my group had mostly first and second graders. One of the kids in my group had a mom that had recently gotten herself off methamphetamines. Unfortunately, when many folks have a victory in their life they assume that they are now a Biblical scholar and although they have never studied the Word of God, or perhaps have even read it, they are quick to judge the walk of others.

Picture if you can, the Sunday after our child's death. We get up earlier than usual because since she went missing we haven't slept through a full night. More than almost anything, I long for a morning when I can get up without being slammed with the knowledge that Jenny is gone. In dealing with extreme grief, you exist in slow motion. Nothing can be done in a hurry, partly because it takes more energy and you need every ounce of strength you have just to keep living, and also because your energy that you do have is used to try to act as normal as possible so you don't upset the people around you. Everyone and I do mean everyone, asks if you are ok! Well gee…let me see…my world as I knew it to be has been destroyed, my God that I trusted would only bring good things into my life, has failed me, my family members cry themselves to sleep at night and the security that I once felt is completely gone! "Yes, thank-you, I'm fine." That said, are you now more comfortable in my presence?

The club was meeting as usual that week and I told

the other leaders that I'd need a couple of weeks off to get my emotions under control. Small people are frightened when adults weep at every turn and I felt that my presence with the kids would not be beneficial. The woman that I mentioned before actually verbally accosted me over my decision to take a break.

"Who do you think you are upsetting the kids like that? They look forward to club nights with you and you are so self absorbed since your daughter died that you can't even manage to keep your commitment to a group of children! You say you believe the Bible and the Bible says that it's the best thing in the world to be in God's presence…if you daughter really did make Jesus her Lord and Savior, then you should be glad that she's dead!" she fumed.

At times like that I tend to be rendered speechless, but she of course was not.

"My dog had puppies last week and one of them didn't make it. Not one person from this church called to offer me help. Not one! They were all absorbed with you. So, if you think you are so awesome to God, maybe you ought to look at the poor example you are and realize that other people have problems too!"

What is it in we humans that makes us think always first about ourselves? Maybe it's our instinct for survival that makes us self centered, but our need to compare our difficulties and even to place them on a rating scale seems endless.

Needless to say, so I don't leave you hanging, she and her child left the church. Lord Jesus, I pray that the leaders of her next church had more luck with training her in the Word than we did.

Unfortunately that was only one of many times that I was the topic of someone's err. After taking a youth group from four kids to thirty five, starting a dance group with them, getting them involved in enough church related activities that they'd have an identity apart from the world, the enemy of our souls once again attacked.

Schools are filled now days with diversity, or permission to not follow God, and free choice, or permission to sin without the accompanying guilt. Having been bombarded with questions about "religious" groups that don't see Jesus Christ as Lord and Savior, I decided to teach on cults. The New Age philosophy that "all is God, God is in us, therefore we are God" permeates society. If in fact all is God, then it stands to reason that a rock can answer your prayers. No, wait; if we are God then we can answer our own prayers. Imagine a frightening moment when we cry out, "please Me, help me!" It just doesn't work. Anyway, to prove my point I had all the kids go out to my front yard, over to an area with a lot of rocks. I jokingly told them to find a rock that they could truly "bond with" and bring it back inside. Ridiculous, right? I proceeded to explain the misinformed premise about the rock being God. We laughed, joked, prayed, and the kids went home. By the next week, the word spread through the church that I was teaching New Age and one boy told his parents that I denounced Christ and told the kids to worship rocks! Now most would say, bless his little lying heart, right? Wrong, this began the back biting, picking apart of Cookie and the process continued for close to a year. One parent wanted to get together for coffee and Phil and I met them at a restaurant. We had just sat down when she brought out a legal pad filled with ought she had against me that started three years prior to this night. I was accused of saying things I'd never said, believing things I didn't believe, and behaving in ways I never had, all the while watching this mother's indignant face as she hurled one accusation after another on me.

Remember the Scripture that tells us not to let the sun go down on our anger? This lady had many days of bitterness built up in her heart. If we agree with Scripture we can also assume that since she chose not to go to me with her complaint when it happened, her offerings to God were ignored.

It would be so simple to let God examine our hearts and our motives before we decide to make someone else our scapegoat for our own lack of peace.

My kids learned a lot from the experience. For months we attended church where everyone in my family was greeted and I was ignored and whispered about. Most would just leave, right? But I had clearly heard the voice of God say, "when the day of evil comes, stand". I'll never forget the morning as we prepared to go to service that Merigen pleaded with me… "Please don't go, Mommy. Those people hate you and they don't want you there!" Hard to find an answer to that.

Even harder is knowing that some of the very people that chose not to follow God's word in this circumstance, who deliberately caused hurt and harm to the body of Christ, later showed up in positions of authority in other churches. I just don't get it. How do you fall on your face before God and still refuse to make peace with your brothers? No wonder we Christians have such bad publicity. We don't need the world to tear us apart…we do just fine on our own.

Years later I became the Senior Pastor of the same church that stoned me. It was just months after Jenny died and I determined that I would hold the church together by the grace of God until He brought the man that was really supposed to pastor these people.

My approach was different from our former pastor, although he implemented many of the same tools. I decided that if we as a body were going to hold together we would need to minister as a team. We experienced fellowship in a non-traditional manner in that we had eighty percent of the church involved in ministry. It was about three years in, that during a prayer time at our Divisional Conference that I cried out to God and asked my now often repeated question… "Where is the pastor for my church?"

"Stop seeking", was God's reply, "I have called you to lead this church so that you can raise boys to be men of God."

You've got to be kidding me, I thought. How long is this going to take? If I knew then what I know now… Well, let's just say that tucking and running might have been an option were it not for Jonah's example when he tried to run from God. Fish food anyone?

"Feed My Sheep"

~ Jesus Christ ~

And so, the boys came to our church. Most arrived because they thought one of the girls in our youth group was cute. They came in, hat twisted sideways, swagger to their walk, either because they thought it made them look cool, or because they had placed the waist of their jeans just below their crotch, I'm not certain. These boys had yet to experience a change of voice, body hair growth, or acne...but they are here and God has given me a directive.

When kids are in mid high or early high school, an optimum opportunity arises to share Christ with them. Actually they are a captive audience because they don't yet drive and their parents figure if Johnny wants to go to "that church thing", it probably can't hurt. We brought them in with tag walls (legal graffiti), break dancing, pool tables, and Cindy's free, and may I say incredible, supper. The girls primped and giggled, the boys walked with a gangster limp and our youth team fasted and prayed. We saw God deliver kids from the hand of Satan over and over again. Witches, with nasty habits of casting spells, Druids, goddess worshippers, Satan worshippers, and everything in between came through our doors to disrupt and confuse, but God used our team to share truth and His plan for each kid would surface. I am convinced that any boy will find something to follow if he sees power, because boys never feel powerful, and if he thinks he can create a rebellious shock response when he announces his allegiance then the age old "you're not the boss of me" gets to reel its ugly, though very predictable head. During prayer one night an extremely short thirteen year old attempted to put me in my place by informing me, in a growly voice, that I didn't know who I was messing with. Scary stuff, right?

We led him to the Lord and watched him grow in the following months. After he broke up with a girl in our youth group, he stopped coming and didn't return calls. A year later I ran into him at a store he was working at and he told me he was now a Hindu. According to him, he liked that better than following Christ. Oh if these kids could get a picture of what they are bartering. Red or green chili? Buddha or Jesus? Our egos will never cease to amaze me!

As a female Senior Pastor, I run into the Mommy hood dilemma fairly regularly. You know what I mean… mom always cuts you a break, she is the queen of second and third and fourth chances, while Dad is the hardnosed "you knew the rules and you broke them so pay up!" part of the equation. I've tried to raise the boys with a mother heart and have discovered that a mother heart is easily broken. I've attempted to be a no nonsense dictatorship and made everyone mad and frustrated, including me. I've directed them believing I was mentoring, but the boys felt controlled. How do you show a tender heart and a firm stand at the same time? Lines are muddied now a days. Men are allowed to cry, have manicures, go to tanning salons, and take dance lessons…to name a few changes. It's now ok to say, "I love you" not just to your girlfriend or wife, but to your brothers as well and with society changing what manly behavior is, training boys to be men of God isn't as easy as it may seem.

I've made some enormous mistakes along the way. When you are in ministry and your kids are part of your ministry, you find, as I did, that there is an ever present circle of fellow believers waiting for you to play favoritism toward your own children. These folks never pull you aside privately to tell you that your child is sexually involved with a member of your youth group…No, they have to scream it at you in front of half the church. So, there…now you're shocked, aren't you? Ha ha…The bigger question is what kind of grown up believers are we training that they would deem it necessary to tear down anyone's family in order to feel superior? We in ministry like to say that God blesses all of us who serve Him and our families as well. Eventually that becomes true, but when you've watched your kids get critiqued, ridiculed, and judged while they are trying to grow up, you've got to wonder why people think that a parent's call to serve is the child's as well; my kids are as prone to sin as yours are. My kids are as chosen and anointed by God as yours are. And my kids have a right to choose their own path as yours do…don't they?

Pastors, male and female, make the choice to wear several different hats in order to serve God. For years I tried to treat my family the same as my congregation. You know what I discovered? The congregation will get bent out of shape and take their marbles and go home (or to another church with better toys), but your family will be with you forever. The priority list taught in many a seminar is truly the way to live as stress free as possible; God first, spouse and kids second (or kids third depending on where you're at in life), and job and ministry last. When I die I pray that people will say that I loved well, not that I preached well.

When I first met Courtney, he was Mr. Cool. He came to youth group with Jon, an already established part of our church. He approached everything as the "world" does as evidence that the first night, he picked out a cute girl and asked her out. She said "no", mostly because she didn't know him at all, and so he kept coming back. Eventually he met God and his life was transformed. The thing that most stands out with Court is that he developed the ability to be truthful. Sounds crazy to say that, but truth is not something that most people pride themselves in.

I've watched him press into God through many heartbreaks and fears over the years and have seen an unbelievable ability to love pour from his heart. There is not a small human on this planet that isn't drawn to Courtney. God's hand is clearly on him.

Mike is also a Mr. Fun Guy. He and Kalie grew up together and had a constant love/hate relationship. Both easily entertained, they terrorized their Christian school, later the home school co-op, and stood through some very rough years together. Mike was the rescuer growing up, always looking out for the underdog because he felt like one so often. He grew up to be a man of faith, a drummer on our Worship Team, and a person still driven toward new adventure.

Jon has always been the behind the scenes friend to all. Slow to speak, he can turn a room into hysterics when his view of life and circumstances surfaces. He has a God given musical ability that has allowed him to intern as a Worship leader at our church and I've no doubt that one day we will all be familiar with his music.

I met Marvin literally on my roof! He had recently moved to New Mexico and Courtney brought him over to help Phil and me with some roof repairs. As usual, they climbed the tree to get on the roof even though for years I had told all of the kids not to or they would fall and break their necks! No one ever listens. I sensed right away that God had brought Marvin to us for a specific reason and I started to pray about him. He is a young man with a sensitive heart that has been through some awful things in his life. For awhile he lived with us and we were able to impart what God wanted to use to begin to heal his heart. Both babies and dogs are drawn to Marvin… you know what that says about his character.

I would love to say that when I first met Shaun I was blessed he wanted to date Merigen, but that wouldn't be true. He fancied himself to be a bit of a gangster and wore his hair slicked back, his pants way low, and he had this look about him when he looked at Merigen like he knew her intimately. "Oh no you don't!" I wanted to scream at him. Thank God that neither of them could drive in ninth grade. I spent most weekends transporting him to our house or her to his. The benefit in all those miles was that he started to come to our church and so I was able to better know him from a spiritual point of view. Does that make sense? When I worship with someone, I feel a kinship that helps me know them better. Anyway…over the years, his family joined us; his brothers were part of our youth group and for a couple of years, our home school co-op. When he was sixteen he gave his life to the Lord, and thus began his Christian walk. Shaun went to Masters Commission for a year when he was seventeen and Merigen remained committed to him while he was away. When he returned, I gave him more responsibility in the church as well as two other young men that had come to Jesus in our fellowship, Stev and Marty.

It was awesome watching them move out in ministry and it gave me the feeling that I was truly fulfilling my commission from God to raise boys to be men of God. I've discovered along the way that certain temperaments mesh with other certain temperaments well. Alas, mine and my now son-in-law, Shaun's did not.

Heading for more pain, Merigen and Shaun and his family left our fellowship to start their own church. I had wanted to build a ministry that my whole family could be part of and now, because I handled ministry direction in this case poorly, I'd pay with the desolation of a unit that we'd spent years building. I've been through several church splits in my time in ministry, but nothing felt like a death to me like this did. Merigen was forced to stand by while those that she loved were once again under attack, but she stood by Shaun and kept her relationship with me through it all. The price we pay for lessons in life is often far higher than it would have been if we'd all seek God's plan instead of making our own.

It's been more than five years now and I still feel the stab of what could have been. I drive by Shaun and Mer's church on the way to mine every Sunday and I wonder if the price I paid was too high. Our relationship is restored, but I don't get to be in Worship with the daughter Phil trained to lead, and I don't get to pray with the son-in-law I helped to raise. But, as I pull myself from musings, I see what God has brought to me in the raising of Marty and Stev.

That story is for another chapter.

"For nothing is impossible with God."

~ Luke 1:37 ~
NIV

Have you ever noticed, I mean really noticed, how when one door closes another one opens? Granted there are times during the closing or the opening that your hand can get smashed in the door and you can end up with bloody pulps where your fingers used to be, but it sure gets your attention. So often in my life I've laid out a great plan that I then presented to God to give His approval on. I've learned however, that God is supposed to be the one to lay out the plan and we are supposed to go along with it!

When the smoke settled after Shaun and Mer left, God truly opened my eyes to what I did have in terms of other leaders that I may not have noticed if my family was still at our church. One of the young women in our church had fallen for a guy that she described to all of us as just perfect. When we did meet this remarkable specimen, we were introduced to a tall, slender young man that looked a great deal like Abraham Lincoln. The thing that struck me about Marty was his eyes. There is warmth and a lack of pretense that emanates from within him. He is easy going, extremely intelligent, and clearly in love with Kimmy.

Ok, let's rally the troops and get this kid saved! God of course, answered that prayer and Marty began to read and study the Word. At first he did some teachings and would help out here and there. But after his first child was born, and the child was completely deaf, a transformation took place that was almost visible...like the changing of a garment. What a great and glorious God we have that can bring wonderful things out of situations meant for despair! The baby had an implant inserted in his ears when he was less than a year old and now, at age eight, he hears as well as any other kid.

But what it did in Marty is what is so remarkable. What Satan wanted to use to bring him down, only made him stronger. By pressing into God during his darkest time, Marty has learned to move forward regardless of circumstances. He is now an Assisting Pastor at our church and is in charge of various ministries as well as having a full time job. Pastor Marty is the one I go to when I need to get anything done that I have neither the time nor the inclination to do. This man has no screaming desire to be recognized as some do. For years I wore myself out trying to make sure that others knew I had value...but for what? God already had been whispering my value in my ear for years and for some crazy mixed up reason, I didn't listen. Hey, that sounds like Solomon as he wrote in Ecclesiastes 4:4, "Again, I saw that for all toil and every skillful work a man is envied by his neighbor. This also is vanity and grasping for the wind." (NKJV) I tell you, sometimes I feel positively enlightened!

Anyway, my point is that I've learned from Marty to allow your actions to speak louder than your words and a greater throng of listeners will assemble.

Stev came to us because of Monica. See my point? Shaun came for Mer, Marty came for Kim, and Stev came for Monica. Clearly to grow a large church in this manner you need a lot of awesome girls! I wonder if that's why there are so many "she planet" type movies? Ok, now I'm concentrating again and I'm ready to tell you about Estevan or Stev as we call him.

This boy became man is what most would say,

short of stature. I mention this only to share another thing I've learned on my life journey so far. Most men, not all, but most, seem bent on stating obvious things as though they are comical new revelations. Brilliant statements such as, "Hey, Dude, you got a tattoo!" I always want to say something like, "No way...did you notice it because it covers his entire arm?" But that seems inappropriate so I just mutter those comments in my head. To Stev someone ALWAYS says, "Really Stev, don't just sit there, stand up! Oh right, sorry, you already are standing!" Ha ha ha...seriously? Do they even hear themselves? Those comments are right up there with my personal favorite addressed to me, "Your name is Cookie? Are you chocolate chip or oatmeal?" Oh just give me a minute to see if I've lost my sense of humor or if it's just that I've heard that like twelve million times in my life! Jeepers, I'm sounding positively cranky. My hope is that those who deliver dialog such as this will please refrain in the future. Loving others includes validating who they are inside and I've met some incredible people whose insides aren't too similar to their outsides.

To the dismay of his family, Stev found Jesus and began to study the Bible like a starving man with a bag of Peanut Butter Cups. Along with his new found faith he proceeded in the art of debate with Monica who has been raised in the Word her entire life. When he came to understand that he couldn't best her, he married her and he is an Assisting Pastor at our church today. He is a person with a gift of administration and has suffered no end of frustration over my inability to stick to some type of flow chart. He memorizes his sermons and has obtained more Biblical knowledge in a few years than most gain in a lifetime.

The Lord added Pastor Juan, our Spanish pastor a few years ago and Brother Clarence, who I'd been praying for over the last several years and who came to a powerful relationship with God when in prison for the last time. For five years he sat at the feet of Jesus through the study of His Word and left prison ready to minister to those that had not been as fortunate as he.

God has been faithful to bring the boys that He would use to further His kingdom, but I've had to learn to let go and let God train them by moving through me. Had I been more of a leader years ago, the path would probably have been less wrought with pain and disappointment, but then too, maybe I wouldn't know what I know now if the journey hadn't been challenging.

Phil and I were sitting at our dining table when the door bell rang and our dogs Naomi and Dakota proceeded to bark their, "Hey, I know you" barks. It was Sunday evening and Mer and Shaun had stopped by to visit. Their church is growing in size now, but more importantly is how God has grown them and us. Shaun has a passion for the Word of God and many times now after a visit, I realize that I've learned from his point of view. Mer is still a strong supporter of him, but clearly has a faith deeply rooted on her own. I look around the table and we're laughing and talking about taking a vacation together and I realize that although none of us would want to go through the pain of the split again, we've all changed for the better as we each in our own way allowed God's Holy

Spirit to teach us and lead us out of bitterness, jealousy, and pain.

What a gift to see that in some small way, when I wasn't making him miserable, I helped to raise Shaun into the man of God he's become. How awesome is that?

"Oh what a tangled web we weave, when first we practice to deceive."

~ Sir Walter Scott 1771-1832 ~

Some moments in life change your perspective forever. I've spoken to women who have experienced physical assault and rape and I know that when your world is shattered, no Christian platitude restores it. There are many forms of rape that I've come to understand. Men and women both experience this tactic of the devil in many different ways.

Years ago, I wrote of a time in my life that held such agony that I felt catapulted back to the time when Jenny was missing.

My world, my life as I knew it, was raped. The assault on love seemed irreversible. I've always desired a haven of safety and I thought I'd created it in my home. Every picture, every throw pillow, and every plant lovingly tended gave me peace. Here in my world, I was safe. But my world was defiled while Phil and I were away. Our youngest was staying at our home with a friend of hers and while I gave my trust with some reserve, I believed that all that she'd been taught would prove itself in our absence. I trusted her to care for, respect, and honor our home while we were away...she raped it and then ran away.

What in all that I tried to fill her heart with caused her to care not one iota for the people her dad and I are? We were attending a church convention in Chicago when Kalie hosted a pot party at our house. When she was discovered by Merigen and Shaun, who were wondering who all the cars in the driveway belonged to, Kalie ran away. She was fifteen years old and she ran to the apartment of a twenty two year old man. No one knew where she was from eight o'clock on the evening of the party until noon the next day when a friend of ours sleuthed her out.

Countless calls were ignored, innumerable pleas left as messages on her cell with no response...why? We thought we were being responsible parents when we provided all our daughters with cell phones so that we could always get a hold of them. Seven years ago we experienced the same hell when Jenny was missing for thirty six hours. She was found floating face down in a flooded field as we paced and prayed and waited. For reasons I'll never understand, another of our kids was missing.

I've been told that we should have watched our youngest better. Somehow, someway, we could have kept her on the right path. A patient's parent in our office once made the proud statement that kids that are in trouble, are obviously not raised in a Christian home. It took all I had not to strangle her! Christianity does not guarantee a trouble free life as though all your time spent in the Word will give your life better blessing for good behavior! Families are made up of different people with their own thoughts, desires, characteristics and such. We can guide our kids in the path God has laid out, but we cannot make them conform...that's up to them. No matter how badly I wanted my beautiful daughter to be pure and innocent for her someday wedding, that wasn't going to be.

When Kalie turned thirteen we began to see a turmoil rise up inside her. It presented often like all other teenage rebellion issues, but I always felt that some of it was rooted in the fact that she'd been adopted. Her desire to connect with her birth mom in a tangible way such as in like behaviors was evident. Kalie was conceived when her birth mom was seventeen and it seemed like Kalie wanted to follow the same path. Hours of professional counseling didn't help, hours of prayer didn't help, and love from us…well, our love certainly didn't prevent the emotional and spiritual violation we experienced.

Can love prevent anything? It doesn't stop lies and pretense, it doesn't create true relationship, and it can't heal. Love is only a force when it's coupled with trust. Simply put, if my relationship with someone is built on lies, it really isn't a relationship because what you've shown me of yourself really isn't you. No wonder the devil uses lies as one of his main "gifts" to mankind. For reasons beyond me, Kalie doesn't want what I have to give and no amount of prayer, pleading, or tears will change that. She is beautiful, talented, and intelligent and she has begun a journey that will ravish her, her family and all her relationships. When a person falls in love with methamphetamines, everyone else takes a back seat.

So, I put my hopes for her away and I clean. For centuries that's what broken women have done. If I move the furniture and wash the windows, my life view will have to become better, right? I attempt to remake the circumstances by changing the set from the one that showed my baby as a drug addict, to the one that has her riding horses and laughing on the swings. I remind myself that God is in control, right? But I still fight the frigid fear that maybe I'm on my own with this one. There must be a lesson to learn, but dear God…I don't know what it is.

Kalie was supposed to go to Denmark as an exchange student for her junior year of high school. Before the Chicago trip incident, I'd though that it would be a good thing for her to get away from negative influences here. We went about notifying the sending organization that she wouldn't be going after all. They wanted us to send her anyway so that her host family wouldn't be disappointed! I wouldn't inflict this pain on anyone else. I'd lived with always wondering if the truth is the whole truth as I watched her lie right to my face and then get offended when I didn't believe her. Her sole purpose at that time was to fuel her desires no matter the cost. She'd wrap herself in delusion thinking she had a right to be offended. We ruined her life when we stopped the exchange student process...how could we invade her privacy like this...she's incredulous that we've taken away her cell phone. She thinks she needs a lifeline to a world of individuals that claim they understand and care, yet when she ran from us, they turned on her to save their own skin.

A lie begins as an easy way out, but it eats like a cancer, removing all traces of truth in all aspects of life. After cancer ravishes an individual it leaves the physical body broken and barren. Each new attack of cancer insurgents removes the essence of what physically was and can only be again, if healing dons it's weapon and invades the intruder. With chemotherapy, a source apart from the body, the assault can begin on the renegade cancer cells that have taken up residence, yet...the battle leaves scars. Weight drops, color drains, hair falls out and blistering sores cover the mucous membranes of the mouth and stomach. What can defeat this intruding army? A person's belief and their will can wage war against the most violent of foe.

The belief that what medical science has discovered will, in the end, kill the invaders and yet leave the host with enough strength to rebuild; and the will of any individual is the greatest weapon they have. The will is what determines the attitude and actions of the occupied host. Only people have the will to trust and believe God. Lies invade and destroy and remove all traces of the person that originally existed. Belief and will can rebuild the individual invaded by deception, but many take an easy path through life and what teenagers call "growing up", we view as an altering of the person God created them to be.

People of faith believe that our all knowing, all seeing God was aware and prepared for this rebellion even before it happened. How I wish He'd told me. And now, all I hear is, "Let Go". I wonder though, how far do I let go? Until she's been gang raped and thrown in a ditch? Until she's arrested and her new friends are all inmates? Does she even fathom what either of those situations will be like? Cold blooded fear, your pulse slams in your ears, eyes stare at first, then dart seeking a way to escape... dry mouth, cold hands...For what? I don't know how to understand this. To be the rebel means to me, bringing the hand of death to your door.

My friends say that a mother's love never leaves you. Perhaps that's true, perhaps it doesn't leave. Yet, right now, I've been crushed so many times, have made my peace so many times, and have cried so many times that this mothers love hides in a vault of protection deep within my soul. You see, I'm the positive one who always finds the bright spot in the tragedy. Having lost one daughter already, I medicate my pain with the knowledge that Jen knew Christ. Through the despair of loss Jen is with the

King of Kings and the Lord of Lords and she, of all of us, knows the end from the beginning.

But this, this with my youngest isn't the swift current of a flood that pulled Jen into the arms of Jesus. This is a churning, angry, whirlpool that threatens to suck life and love into a deep, black hole. As she spins in her turmoil, arms flailing, crying out at times, I notice too that this child, at times, laughs at the sheer thrill of the terror. There are no answers in the depth of me. I'm the peacemaker...the fixer...But I've been given no tools for this.

My heart breaks as I watch Merigen as her sister spirals. She asks the questions I think everyone does. What could she have done differently? Was this because she got married and wasn't home anymore? Was it because Kalie was adopted? Why is she doing this to us? Why is God allowing this? Haven't we been through enough? I pray that I'll find the words to heal the disappointment and fear in Mer, but the answers I need are the same ones she needs. I wish there was a way to know when life was going to come crashing down.

There's a place in time when you see yourself about to become a victim. The car speeds forward into the blackness of night with only two small headlights to guide your way. But fog rolls in and the headlights almost seem more of a hindrance than a help. Specks move into your vision and the strain of seeing the road ahead tenses every muscle. Hoping the road ahead is straight, you barrel forward only to discover there is a hairpin turn in the road ahead. Too late. Too late. You attempt the brakes, but your timing is wrong and you lose control and crash into the unknown. Adrenaline surges through your body for quite some time, but then, an eerie calm fills your senses. All you want to do is sleep...escape... get away.

How could this have happened?

"Now what?"

~ Cookie ~

Up until very recently, Kalie has insisted that Merigen is the "perfect child". Of course we have always refuted such claims. Any parent will tell you that each and every one of your kids is the perfect "them". But has this journey of life so far been easier with Merigen? In some ways it has because for whatever reason, through church splits and family disasters, through death, disappointment, and pain, she has held fast to the Gospel of Jesus Christ. She knows where her true north rests and because she has lived through more pain than most people her age, she has embraced the height, depth, and breadth of the love of God. Mer is a total mix of Phil and me. She has her dad's passion for worship and the voice to go with it, but she also has the ability to make something from nothing like me. Her optimism is similar to mine and when she's been hurt…the pain penetrates deeply. To say to Merigen, "just forget about it" would be like asking her to stop breathing. She won't hold a grudge, but she will dissect a comment until she is certain that the true meaning behind it has been discerned.

I've watched her deal with Kalie's' drug and alcohol addiction over the years and as much as it broke my heart to see Kalie throw herself away, it hurt as much to see Merigen struggle for solid footing while her sister walked away from everything Merigen holds dear. Through it all, Merigen has placed the burden upon herself, of never disappointing her dad and me because we've been through enough. How do you help a child realize that she has no responsibility for what we've experienced? All of us make our own choices and all of us pay the price for those choices. I've come to realize that no matter how unruly our kids can become, the dream for who they can be resides deep within a parent heart and we will always find a way to look for good in seeming disaster.

After years of intermittent homelessness, us rescuing, Kalie running, jail time, and treatment options, Kalie finally got caught in a big way and faced possible prison time. Odd to say, but we were all relieved. If she was in prison at least we'd know where she was and if she kept her mouth shut, she'd probably live through it. It will never cease to amaze me how angry those that engage in criminal activity are when they get caught. She'd name call and cuss a blue streak and try to show us how bad the system is, but all along we were praising God that maybe it was finally over!

Fear does crazy things in some people and it caused Kalie to quit using methamphetamines. Slowly the pick marks healed on her face and she put on some weight. After a couple of months we'd notice that she was cleaner and the metallic odor that addicts think no one can smell, was gone. We still were responding to middle of the night phone calls, still getting her and her boyfriend food, and still listening and only half believing what she'd say, but things were improving. Through all of this, Merigen would attempt to form relationship with Kalie and for a time she'd succeed but then something would trigger Kalie and she'd be off again. During her sobriety from meth she smoked an enormous amount of weed and drank profusely. Some folks think that an addict can just stop everything cold turkey and skip along with their life. Nothing could be further from the truth. A person that uses any chemical to deal with life will have to learn to face normal human emotions without the drug of choice to take the raw feelings away. In an answer to prayer,

Kalie was sentenced to drug court and this was what would help to change her life.

In our county drug court is a year long process that includes urine tests on demand, group counseling, individual counseling, securing employment, and weekly consultation with the judge. If any infraction of the program occurs the participant goes to jail. Kalie pressed in with all she had and quit weed and alcohol. She embraced the second chance, or hundredth chance, and truly got clean. She returned to church, attends recovery group, and is planning on college within the next year. What has blessed us is the honesty she expresses because now we actually do know what's going on.

Merigen and Kalie are finally forming the relationship that sisters hope to have. To say that we all lived happily ever after would be premature. When you have dealt with addiction and repeated affronts to you relationship with someone, you can't help but wonder, "What now?" Or, "when is the other shoe going to drop?" As parents, we believe that if we follow the life manual to a letter our children will be practically perfect in every way... like Mary Poppins. I've come to realize that there are no perfect parents and no perfect children and no matter how much love you pour into someone, they will still walk their own path.

As a pastor I am continually dumbfounded by those that attempt to appear holy and righteous yet live with sin and sorrow at home in private. Addiction permeates our churches and unless we are willing to address the issues surrounding abuse in all forms, we will create huge social clubs that have nothing to do with a people set apart by God.

What does the Lord require of us, but to live justly, love mercy, and walk humbly with our God?

Sometimes though, I'd rather smack someone as say hello!

"The fruit of the Spirit is
love, joy, peace, patience,
kindness, goodness, faithfulness,
gentleness, self-control; against
such things there is no law."

~ Galatians 5:22-23 ~
ESV

If those of us, who consider themselves new creations in Christ, would walk out our lives as though we are new, the draw to this life called Christianity would be irresistible. So many times I've witnessed one confessing Christ as Savior while bowing down to their own flesh. I've done it myself. When the kids were little they attended a Christian school where I worked as a PE teacher and Drill Team coach. There was a young man that worked there that was the son in law of the principal. The young man was a teacher of something, but I don't recall what. He continually attempted to tell me what to do as though he was my boss.

One day I dismissed my class early to the gym so that they could have some time before Drill practice. I'm talking maybe five minutes, when (I'll call him Mr. Smith) Mr. Smith literally storms out of his classroom yelling at me to stop right there and what did I think I was doing by dismissing my class early! I explained why and continued to walk away. He chased after me telling me how irresponsible I was being, blah, blah, blah. I'd held my "self-control" long enough and with utmost drama I uttered what I thought God thought of him, threw open the door for my exit, because I knew the slam would make my point, and the door slowly hummed its way back to closure. I picked the door that closed automatically and softly. What a disappointment that my slamming exit was thwarted! However, as I got in my car to go "cool off" the Lord reminded me that I was called to be an example of the fruit of the Spirit in my life regardless of what others did. What a lesson to learn.

That lesson has served me well when I've sought a hiding place in the Spirit through accusations and threats.

Threats? Oh yes. The, "if you don't remove so and so from your council immediately, I'll have you fired!" And, "if you don't let me speak from the pulpit, I'll tell everyone what a witch you are!" Oh the joys some days hold! There was a council meeting at my home where I was informed that one person was, "the voice of the people" and the people only felt okay sharing with him because I wasn't listening. Numerous times in my Christian walk when screaming would have been stress relieving, but the times that I have screamed only left me feeling like I'd failed. Besides, one man had already criticized me for being too emotional in the pulpit. Screaming would certainly be unacceptable.

Over the years I've heard how blessed people feel with their churches and their lives in general. What I don't understand is why if everyone is so happy are they constantly picking at others like a bunch of vultures at a buffet? How it must break the heart of God. Granted, it is easier to talk about what someone's doing wrong instead of actually praying for them and bringing them some support! Did Jesus really mean for us to cookie cutter ourselves and our congregations when he spoke of love? Or are we supposed to seek and know His love so completely that to act apart from the fruit of the Spirit would be like wearing someone else's skin.

I want to see people as Christ does. I want to look for potential instead of faults and I want to touch the heart of God through my prayers. In September 2010, Phil and I, along with four others from our fellowship, went to Haiti on a short term medical mission trip. The aftermath from the earthquake was devastating; tarps, tents, and cardboard don't dot the landscape...they are the landscape. There are people everywhere and the United Nations peacekeeping forces are everywhere. Some of the people are dressed to the nines and some aren't clothed at all. Many of the children have on just a shirt with a bare bottom. The heat is stifling and the smells are foreign. The people were drinking out of muddy streams and rivers, bathing and washing clothes and animals in the water as well.

Some of the orphanages house forty or more kids ranging in age from infant through teenage. They have one meal a day of a fried cornmeal done on a charcoal flame. Their restroom may be an outhouse, or the corner of a room. They run at you, not to you. The kids want to see your reaction to them before they offer a piece of their heart to you. I notice immediately how few of the infants and toddlers even cry. They may whimper, but I'd guess that when your cries go unanswered you simply stop trying. Many of the little ones have worms, most are malnourished, and some were pulled from rubble after the earthquake. All, without a doubt, are survivors...not just physically, but emotionally as well.

Having control issues like I do, I proceed to redo their lives in my mind. My thoughts go something like this; if we clean all the concrete and paint Big Bird on the walls, and wash the sheets, and build a kitchen, and have story time, and give them three balanced meals a day, than the kids will be happy. But, happiness comes from belonging and mattering to someone and not so much from things that surround.

In prayer that night I asked God how we could possibly make life better for the people of Haiti and He asked me, "Why are you trying to Americanize Haiti?" Oops! I guess as often as I've preached that the United States doesn't have the corner on correct Christianity, I forgot to put my convictions into practice. I determined to change my mind and instead of helping them be more like us, I wanted to learn to be somewhat like them. The end result of that school was learning to embrace the moment. Sometimes just noticing a person can mean everything to them. I confronted my own shallow approach to what should be done in what way while in Haiti. I enjoyed the freedom of being able to be present in the moment without concerning myself with the expected outcome. And the time there forever changed me.

You see, even before the writing of this book became possible, I've been trying to understand why I've lived the life I've lived. I guess I'm writing it to give those of you that have struggled along in life a hope for tomorrow. You see, right now today, my daughters are awesome, my sons in laws are blessed, and my spiritual sons are following God. I've never been more in love with my husband or more at peace with the family of my church. And I've come to understand that every person that has crossed my path has given me an opportunity to see a bit more of the personality of God. I've only ever wanted a secure sense of family and my glorious God has given me exactly that. I truly know that I'm never alone.

So now, I try to look at each occurrence in my life as another opportunity to grow into the person I will one day become. I want to be a better listener and a stronger prayer warrior and I hope to one day be free of control. I often ask myself why I want everyone to do things my way. I mean seriously, have I done my life thus far the best way possible? My own arrogance amazes me.

Ultimately, my goal is to learn to bear with others, be present in the moment, press in to God, and bluntly put...shut up! Except of course when the next thing in my life causes me to scream, "You've got to be kidding!"

Faithful (My Shepherd)

Surely Your goodness
Surely Your goodness
Will follow me all the days of my life
Down the darkest roads
Through the longest storms
You comfort me.

You're faithful to deliver me
To your quiet streams and fields of green
My soul finds rest in You.

Surely Your mercy
Surely Your mercy
Will follow me all the days of my life
In the darkest days
Through the longest nights
You comfort me

And I will dwell, in the house of the Lord forever!

Scott Brownson
©2011Mount Hawley Music/ASCAP ARR
www.scottbrownsonmusic.com

CPSIA information can be obtained at www.ICGtesting.com
Printed in the USA
LVOW062148121011

250198LV00001B/2/P